MW00785067

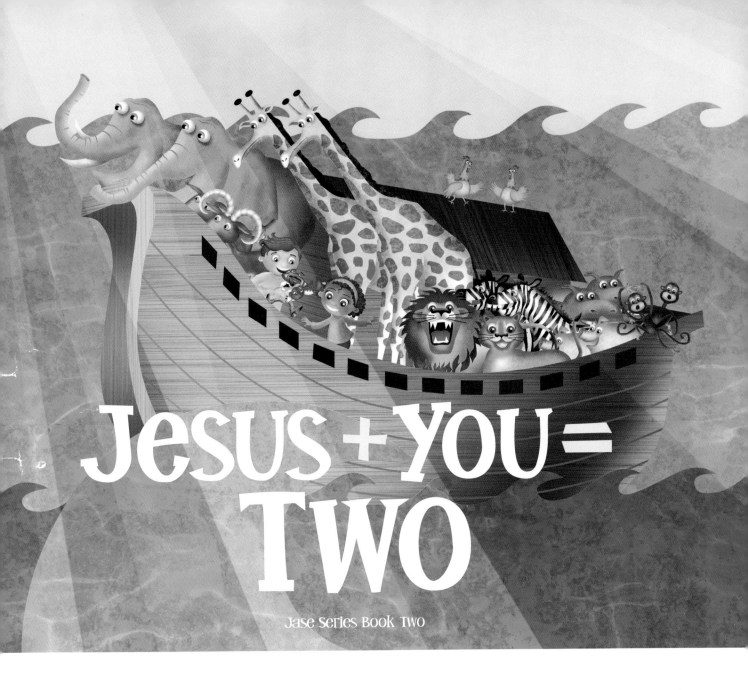

Jesus + You = Two

Jase Series Book Two

Written by Jason Crabb

Illustrated by Anita DuFalla

Copyright © 2013 — Jason Crabb Ministries, LLC

All rights reserved. This book or any portion thereof may not be reproduced or used in any manner whatsoever without the express written permission of the author except for the use of brief quotations in a book review.

Printed in the United States of America   ISBN 978-0-9888994-0-7   www.jasoncrabb.com

The JASE Series is dedicated to my girls: my beautiful wife, Shellye,
and our precious daughters, Ashleigh and Emma. You mean the world to me.
With love from our family to yours:
Jason, Ashleigh, Shellye, and Emma.

Special thanks to Philip and Tina Morris and Donna Scuderi for your creative input and love of the cause.

Number

2

The 2nd Commandment

Friend and crab,
while you love them,
always see
God above them.

1. Love God more than all, even crabs great and small.

2. Friend and crab, while you love them, always see God above them.

3. Don't be crabby toward God. Say His name with your love.

4. God's day of rest is for you — and for your crab, too.

5. All children and crabs, respect Mom and Dad.

6. Don't hurt one another, not a crab or your brother.

7. Crab or person alike: love your husband or wife.

8. Never steal from your brother, your crab, or another.

9. Little boys, girls, and crabs, tell the truth and be glad.

10. Be sure to enjoy your stuff and your crab, not wishing for something your neighbor has.

Jase and his friend Evan were walking
just outside as Evan pointed.

"That's where she lives, I mean, Maya, my friend.
Her father's a soldier in Afghanistan.
Down that hill and across the lawn,
that's her window, with the nightlight on."

Just as Jase turned, ready to go,
came a blinding flash and thunderbolt.

C-R-A-C-K!
went the noise,
shaking the ground,
and Jase went tumbling
down...down...down.

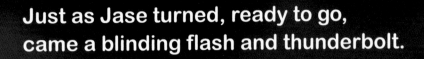

"Remember" said Evan, waving his hands,
"Maya is hurting. She misses her dad."

5

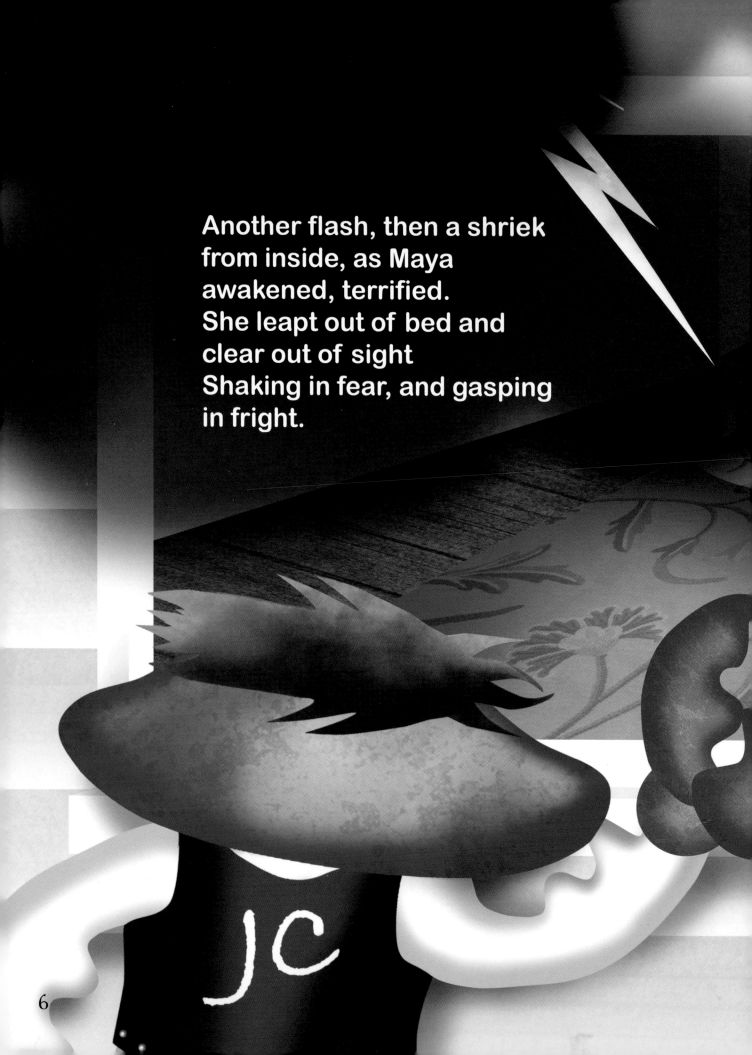

Another flash, then a shriek
from inside, as Maya
awakened, terrified.
She leapt out of bed and
clear out of sight
Shaking in fear, and gasping
in fright.

She dove straight into her mother's arms, who asked her,
"Honey, what is wrong?"

"Oh Mommy! The storm! I'm so afraid.
I wish Daddy were home to stay."

"Jesus is here even when Daddy's gone.
He's keeping us safe during the storm."

"You're right, Mommy, I know that's true.
I guess we've got some sleeping to do!"

Mom walked with Maya back down the hall,
and tucked her in bed with her baby doll.
She kissed Maya's cheek and left her to rest,
as Jase sat quietly in the toy chest.

Maya saw him and asked, "Oh…who are you?
Why are you here, and what do you do?"

"My name is Jase. I have something to say
that will help your fears just crumble away."

"See, God gives us grace. It's more
than enough.
His strength is all ours. We don't
have to be tough."
(1 Corinthians 12:9)

10

"That sounds really cool, but what does it mean, when lightning and thunder frighten me?"

"His power is yours,
whatever the need."

"Oh, Jase, tell me more!"

"Well, certainly!
When scary things happen,
His courage steps in,
so you can be sure you're
safe with Him.

Jesus plus you equals two.
You're *never* alone.
And when you feel weak, He remains strong."

The sky flashed again and a

BOOM!

shook the room.

Maya dove down,
dragging Jase
with her, too.

"Why we're under the bed,
I don't really know.
Remember, Maya, who's guarding this home."

"My dad always says that, but he's far away.
The storm is right here and I'm still afraid."

"Maya, someone much bigger than Dad is here —
Jesus helps *Dad* to rise above fear.

You love your Dad. You show it each day
But see God above him, even when he's away."

"That's the second commandment," Maya said with a smile,
"from God to every crab and child."

"That's right, little Maya. You're getting it now! Let's see how it works. I'll show you how. Did Dad ever tell you about Noah's Ark?" We can go see it. It's not very far."

"I heard of you, Noah, but why are you here
with so many animals, all in pairs?"

"We're here," Noah said, "just as God planned.
A storm is coming to flood all the land.
It's bringing the end of the world that we knew.
But inside the Ark, we'll be saved, two by two."

"Oh, Jase! Raindrops bigger than cats and dogs!"

"We're safe," said Jase, as God sealed the door.

"The waters are rising. The waves are so strong. Jase, how can these animals ever hold on? How can we sleep here? Can we survive? How will God manage to keep us alive?"

"Don't worry, Maya, the ending is good.
God's every promise is faithful and true.
But the ride is still rough, and not easy to take.
In the midst of it all, we'll rely on God's grace."

Jase added a hint of what was to come:
"A dove will go out to check on the flood.
When it returns with a leaf in its mouth,
Noah will know that the water's gone down.
When the dove flies again and doesn't return,
He will know that the flood is gone from the earth."

"Noah, don't worry!"
Maya proclaimed.
"Jase said the end
of the story is great!
This storm will soon
end. The sun will
soon shine..."

"And a rainbow will
spread across the sky.
It's the sign of His
promise," Jase said,
and it's true,
"for everyone here and
everywhere too!"

Suddenly, Jase and Maya were home,
and Maya exclaimed, "Look, Jase—the sun!"

Jase answered and said, "Every storm ends,
and joy and peace always come back again."

Then Maya's mom yelled up the stairs, "Breakfast is ready, Maya my dear!"

Maya and Jase were hungry and ran, while Mom flipped pancakes out of the pan.

"It's grocery day and we're running late,"
said Mom as the pancakes fell onto their plates.

"It's okay, Mom, God will provide whatever we need, whether safety or time."

Mom said, to Jase, "And who might you be?"

"My name is Jase. Evan sent me."

"Great—can you help us finish our chores?"

"I'd love to," said Jase, "and I'll help at the store."

When they got to the market,
Maya told Mom
all the cool things she
learned from the flood.

"God never leaves us. He's
always there.
I hope I can tell someone
else how He cares."

Just then an orange rolled toward their feet.
And a woman cried out, "Please catch it for me."

Jase said to Maya, "Now tell her the news,
about how God loves her the way He loves you."

Maya said sweetly,
"This is for you.
Did you know that God
loves me and you too?"

A giant tear from the
woman's eye
rolled down her cheek
and moistened her
smile.
Another mom and her
son looked on,
but he looked very
sad for someone so
young.

28

Maya told Jase, "He's always that way.
I know you can help him. You'll know what to say."

When they got to the checkout, Jase saw his chance.
He said, "My name is Jase," and held out
his hand.

"Can I help you bag your groceries today?"
The boy said, "Sure, if Mom says it's okay."

When his mom said, "Yes," the packing began,
and when it was finished Jase jumped in the bag.

**Where is he going? Just wait and see.
He'll tell you the story in Book Number Three!**

Jase® — A "Crabb" With a Mission

Children are precious — to us and to God! And their growing-up years are so important to the people they become. Through their everyday experiences, children discover their individual identities, their unique destinies, and the reality of their loving Creator.

When faced with challenges and disappointments, children are comforted to learn that other children share many of the same experiences. As they hear other children's stories, they are strengthened in discovering that they are not alone, or "more strange," or "less courageous" than their peers.

The vision for The Jase® Series took root in my heart two decades ago. Now, as a husband and the father of two beautiful girls, I long to reach children and those who love and care for them with the Good News—the gospel of Jesus Christ! I pray that this children's story will sing the melody of God's heart to you, whatever your age.

— Jason Crabb

coming up next in the Jase series

In this continuing dreamland adventure, Jase® and his friend, Mateo, see Jesus at the Last Supper ... and Mateo learns how three days can change *everything!*

Hey kids!

Now that you've read the book, how would you like to:

- ■ Download Jase FUN pages;
- ■ Access the Jase and You Review
- ■ Earn a diploma from Jase University
- ■ And more ...

Go with me to **WWW.jasecrabb.com** to continue our journey together!!!